#Resist

"Poems of R

By: Nilesh Vasave

Dedication

To each and everyone who are being oppressed, marginalised, abused, castigated, left behind, wrongly persecuted based on their caste, colour, creed, class, race, religion, language, country, ethnicity, sexuality, belief, disability, history and any other way of discrimination. It's time to #resist.

INDEX

Introduction

The idea of resist came to me since last year, when world around me changed upside down on the fateful day of 24th June 2016. The day after the EU referendum vote, where United Kingdom decided to isolate itself and instead of looking into bright future and brotherhood among fellow Europeans, decided to become little England, and go back to past and live in nostalgia, and the event followed that historic mistake. Where suddenly each and everyone of us migrant felt we are not welcome here anymore, we are the enemy and friends started reporting being verbally abused because their ethnicity, religion, country of origin or accents. A kid was killed because he was polish, Burqua ripped off from a british muslim woman's head. Hate massages sprayed on polish people's houses and cars. While all of this going on, across the pond America was busy electing a monster called Donald Trump, which came to power on the promises which will make Hitler proud. Building walls, banning people from countries, building more weapons, taking away healthcare from vulnerable people, rip apart environmental treaties, giving tax breaks to himself and his billionaire friends, stripping away rights of women to choose what's right for their bodies, rights of minority and LGBTQ communities, and rise of anti immigrants, anti refugees sentiments across the world and specially in Europe. The rise of far right and neo Nazis (will not use the softer term "alt-right"), and the violence and hatred that followed.

All of these events and everyday seeing how the world is changing for worse made me realise, I can't sit silent. I must not sit silent and be a spectator. I must do something. I must scream. I must shout. I must say "stop it!" This is not normal. This must change. I must Resist. Resist. Resist. Resist. And my sincere hope is you, the reader, and everyone who feels the same as me, every decent folk who wants to change the world for better, we all unite and #RESIST.

Before I conclude, I would like to take this opportunity to thank my dear friend, Franziska Liebig for editing and providing critique for my poems.

With these sentiments, I present to you my poems of resistance. Hope you like it. Spread the word. Spread the resistance.

Refugees

They are scared, they are hurt.

They are not vermin; why are you throwing dirt?

They are tired, they are hungry.

They are not terrorists; why are you angry?

They are human, they are us.

Why are you throwing them under the bus?

The boats are heavy; water is pouring.

Their cries for help, you are blatantly ignoring.

Why are you silent? A human being, each -

A dead child lying face down on a golden sandy beach.

Smash the patriarchy

Women you are strong, you are smart

This is the mission statement,

We should take it all to heart

Smash the patriarchy

Break that glass ceiling

Kill that gender pay gap

And start all the healing..

From brexit to border wall,

From climate to healthcare for all..

The system is fair for all,

It's our time, it's our call

Let's do it together,

All the sistas, brothas and othas..

Who call themselves feminista,

or just a decent human fella

Singing, shouting, chanting

Marching, protesting, politicking

Let's all say it together

Smash the patriarchy

Break that glass ceiling

Kill that gender pay gap

And start all the healing..

We are not done

We may be scattered, but we are one

Not really whole, but more than our sum

They might be many, but they are numb

Though they can't hear us, we are not dumb

Nothing will stop us, not even a gun

We are just starting, we are not done

You're not alone - join us now, come!

Stand Up!

Stand up!

Yes, you! Stand up!

Against hate,

No time to waste,

It's your fate!

Stand up, come on, Stand up!

Against oppression, bigotry, against the state!

No time to sleep,

Get up and tear down that iron gate!

Stand up, and shout

Those slogans and those chants,

No time to waste, no time to doubt,

Don't listen to those hateful rants.

Stand up today, stand up now!

Use your voice, make it known

or lose all right to ever moan;

Don't complain, don't ever cry,

How did this happen - why oh why?

#Resist : Poems of resistance

Nilesh Vasave

Breath

My taxes are up!

The corporation, the VAT, the GST.

Earning my dollar, my dimes throughout the year,

While the tax man sips his camomile tea.

No jobs, cut the social services,

Privatise the NHS, close the border,

Stop the child refugees,

Check their teeth!

BREATH!!!

Britain will be great again.

World will trade again.

Rich will buy again,

the apartments which will be empty as their souls.

Corporations will be fed again,

The healthy diet of tax breaks.

Billions of tax breaks.

Trickled down effect, you see?

It's economy stupid!

What else can it be?

Money spent by billionaires, investments by corporations creates jobs,

Jobs feeds people, people buy more products,

Products, in terns profits the corporations,

#Resist : Poems of resistance

Nilesh Vasave

Corporations which make their owners billionaire,

who will be buying the government with their perfect hair,

So that the government can tell us,

they contribute and deserve somehow… more?!!

While the fair tax payers like us, are treated as a spent whore!

Fucked, and sucked and sucked and fucked,

While billionaires and corporations exploits the loopholes,

And the Government conveniently forgets what is their roles?

Let me remind you,

It's

FOR the people,

And not IGNORE the people.

It's

By the people,

And not LIE to people.

Rise

From the depth of despair,

The treatment which was unfair.

I will rise, rise like a phoenix,

Rise like a morning sun.

From the feelings of hurt,

Bruised and bleeding lying on the dirt.

I will rise, rise like a hulk,

Rise like a tsunami

From the sea of sadness,

Among all this madness,

I will rise, rise like The One,

Rise until I am done.

Alright

am down but I am right,

will win, this bloody fight.

The air is heavy,

The night's cold.

I may be hurt,

I may be old.

Sun will shine,

with the golden light.

Ending this misery,

the cold cold night.

I am hopeful, I am bright.

The truth is with me, and I am alright.

Spirit of my soul

The old neem tree in my yard,

Standing silent, but strong..

Observing all, but keeping all in..

The wind, the sun, the rain and the heat

Nothing can wither, nothing can beat.

Time is growth, time is teacher.

Time can heal, time is preacher.

Showing me truth, showing me life..

Never goes back, it's just gonna fly..

making me frail, making me older,

but teaching me patience, making me stronger

This road is treacherous, my journey seems longer..

but more I endure, more I go deeper

deep and strong, these roots of my soul,

enriched with love, but, pain makes it whole.

Time is passing, the silence has grown,

Strong and steady, standing on my own.

The wind, the sun, the rain and the heat..

Nothing can wither, nothing can beat,

The spirit of my soul.

#Resist : Poems of resistance

Nilesh Vasave

One last shot

I am down, I am tired, I am bruised.

I am sick, I am hurt, I am screwed.

The clouds getting darker,

The rain bit heavier.

The storm of intolerance,

is wrecking havoc on my soul.

The tyranny, the bigotry, the fake news.

Truth, humanity, compassion has no use.

The battle seems over,

My weapons seems blunt.

But, the fire is still burning,

The ember still hot.

Let me summon,

The last bit of courage,

And Fire this one last shot.

Nilesh Vasave

48 Percent

We are 48 percent

Not gone, Not mute

We are here, we are present

Politics of division,

Rhetorics of fear,

Costing us a lot,

Costing us very dear

A bus full of lies,

Those xenophobic cries,

4 percent is not a mandate,

To tear apart our lives.

If things seems broken,

And confidence is shaken,

No need to end it.

Stop. Breath. Think it through.

And Let's try to mend it.

Instead of this stupid, divisive

downright wrong fucking brexit.

#Resist : Poems of resistance

Nilesh Vasave

Mother E.

Mother earth is getting hurt,

While the leaders of freeworld,

The industrialists, trample over each other

to dig that precious golden dirt.

Penning that lucrative deal

Not caring,

Who will suffer, who will heal?

The poor, the voiceless, the young

Inhaling that toxic fumes in their lung.

The voice of reason is drowning fast,

While Mother Earth's taking her breath, last.

Will we listen or will we still drill?

Will we take action or will we kill?

Tell me you will stop it, you can feel.

It's time to stop hurting,

Stop pretending and

Scrap that hurtful, dodgy deal.

Resist : Poems of resistance

Nilesh Vasave

Cancer

The world has cancer

It's called human

A virus so dangerous

Who spares none

The trees are screaming

The birds are weeping

Rivers run dry

Mother Earth cry

While the wheels of progress

Trample the forest

The greed of men

Doesn't give a rest

The nuclear weapons,

Pointing at each other

In the hands of trigger happy maniac

It's not hard to imagine

It doesn't take a brainiac

We are the cancer, we are the virus.

Peace through Strength

Donald Trump said,

"Peace through strength".

I agree with him!

Yes, Peace through strength.

Strength through Unity,

Unity through Diversity,

Diversity through tolerance,

Tolerance through acceptance,

Acceptance through understanding,

Understanding through dialogue,

Dialogue through contact,

Contact through efforts,

Efforts through compassion,

Compassion through love,

Love thy neighbour.

Know thy neighbour,

Knowledge is Power.

And Power means strength.

So, yes! I agree with Donald Trump.

"Peace through Strength"

#Resist

Resist resist resist

The tyranny, the fascism, hate

Spread spread spread

The love, compassion, debate

Oppose oppose oppose

The bigotry, the division, wall

Embrace embrace embrace

The differences, the refugees and all

Fight fight fight

The racism, the sexism, ban

Believe believe believe

In Peace, each other, we can

#Resist : Poems of resistance

Nilesh Vasave

Superhero

I am a Superhero!

Yes, I am..

Getting out of my bed,

When trump is on my tail.

Those xenophobic headlines,

In that awful daily mail..

The colour of my skin, brown as a dirt,

Taking all abuses, hiding all the hurt.

Landing on an airport, standing in a queue

Why are you here? What you gonna do?

Make you doubt yourself, Asking who you are?

Laughing at my accent, mocking in the bar.

Are you lost, sonny? Why have you come this far?

Learn the language, wear the tie.

See a burqa? SCREAM.. we're all gonna DIE!

It's out of control, we need to fix it..

FUCK this EU, we need to Brexit.

Lets go back, make US greater,

Stop these refugees, those Polish, all muslims are traitor.

Smiling with my colleagues, laughing with my friends,

Hiding that sinking feeling, watching all these trends.

Facing all this heat, with all of my might..

Hoping, nay, praying! one day, all this be alright.

With eyes getting heavy, time to put on my cape..

Resist : Poems of resistance

Nilesh Vasave

Pulling up the duvet, preparing to fight that orange shape…

Telling myself..

I am a Superhero!

Yes, I am..

I am an Immigrant Man!

Welcome 45

A tyrant, a bigot, a racist is coming to town

All the decent folks are angry,

No one is happy, it's reason to frown.

Whatever your religion, sexuality or colour

Muslim, transgender or brown

Let's all get together, screaming from our lungs.

Marching, protesting, walking hand in hand

Showing him, showing the world, warning their ilk,

Stop this xenophobia, the racism, the hate.

Or this visit of his will be the beginning of his end.

Humankind

The world is full of people,

Beautiful people, inside and out.

Try to love them first, oh, I insist.

Surrender to love, do not resist.

Love is the cure, it will surely heal -

So open your heart and allow yourself to feel

Now, dig deep, and there you shall find

A world full of hope; beautiful humankind.

#Resist : Poems of resistance

Nilesh Vasave

Printed in Great Britain
by Amazon